LEADERS OF
ANCIENT ROME

CICERO | Defender of the Republic

LEADERS OF
ANCIENT ROME

CICERO
Defender of the Republic

Fiona Forsyth

B
CIC
$ 25.00

I would like to dedicate this book to
Albert Ng of my Latin class.

Published in 2003 by The Rosen Publishing Group, Inc.
29 East 21st Street, New York, NY 10010

Copyright © 2003 by The Rosen Publishing Group, Inc.

First Edition

Library of Congress Cataloging-in-Publication Data

Forsyth, Fiona.
Cicero: defender of the Republic / Fiona Forsyth.— 1. ed.
p. cm. — (Leaders of Ancient Rome)
Includes index.
Summary: Discusses the life and times of the famous Roman statesman and orator, Cicero.
ISBN 0-8239-3590-6 (alk. paper: hbk.)
1. Cicero, Marcus Tullius—Juvenile literature. 2. Statesmen—Rome—Biography—Juvenile literature. 3. Orators—Rome—Biography—Juvenile literature. 4. Rome—Politics and government—265–30 B.C.—Juvenile literature. [1. Cicero, Marcus Tullius. 2. Statesmen. 3. Orators. 4. Rome—History—Republic, 265–30 B.C.] I. Title. II. Series.
DG260.C5 F68 2002
937'.05'092—dc21
                                    2001004764

Manufactured in the United States of America

CONTENTS

ITALY AT THE TIME OF CICERO

● Luca

ETRURIA

ITALIA

Roma

● Tusculum

● Arpinum

Astura ●

Via Appia

Formiae ●

● Puteoli

SARDINIA

MEDITERRANEAN SEA

Lilybaeum ●

SICILIA

● Syracusae

INTRODUCTION: A TIME OF CHANGE

Ancient Rome has been portrayed in films and on television as a rather glamorous world populated by handsome gladiators, evil emperors, and beautiful women. But if you had lived in the Roman Empire during the first century BC, life would have borne little resemblance to this world. The empire had millions of people living in it, from France to North Africa to the Middle East, and the only thing all these people would have had in common was that they were ruled by a city in central Italy: Rome. Most inhabitants of the Roman Empire would never see Rome, let alone enjoy a colorful and glamorous life. And yet, if you were lucky enough to be male, wealthy, well-born, and expensively educated, you might have been caught up in the exciting and eventful politics of Rome. The influence and rights of

The Temple of Vesta (also known as the Temple of Hercules the Victor) was the site of the Roman cattle market. The temple features a Greek design and a marble exterior finish. It was a very expensive structure, and it is symbolic of the wealth that was flowing into Rome by 200 BC.

women, poor people, and slaves were, as you will see, limited.

Rome had grown from its foundation (tradition says that the city was founded in 753 BC) into the most powerful place in the Mediterranean. By building up a large and well-drilled army, Rome had conquered many lands, which were then called provinces. Roman officials were sent out to govern those provinces, and taxes were raised and sent back to Rome. The city was therefore very rich and very powerful. For the inhabitants of Rome, wealth and birth counted a great deal. The official class of the population into which you were born was determined by the amount of money and property owned by your family. If you were lucky enough to be born into one of the wealthiest families, you were a patrician. Everyone else was a plebeian.

In the first century BC, Rome was going through a change from republic to empire. As a republic, Rome had been controlled by her wealthiest citizens, who ruled through the Senate. Now, through her armies, many men saw opportunities to make themselves powerful as individuals rather than as servants of Rome, and these ambitious people clashed with each other. Over a period of fifty years, these clashes led to war. Eventually one ambitious man beat all his rivals and became the sole ruler of Rome. When he died, his heir took over, and so the system of one-man rule was established. We call these rulers emperors.

The first of these emperors, Augustus, once saw one of his grandsons reading a book. The boy appeared to be scared and tried to hide the book, so Augustus took it from him and started to read

A bust of Marcus Tullius Cicero (106–43 BC), Roman statesman, orator, and philosopher

it himself. After some time, he gave the book back, saying of its author, "He was a clever man, my child; and he loved his country."

Augustus was talking about Marcus Tullius Cicero, author of that book and many others. Why then was his grandson so scared to be seen reading a book by Cicero? Perhaps it was because the boy knew how Cicero had died. He had been executed on the orders of three men: Mark Antony, a powerful general; Lepidus, who also had control of a large army; and Augustus himself. This was at a time of great upheaval, and these three men had decided that they were going to divide the control of Rome between them and that the only way to achieve this was to murder all their opponents first. Augustus's grandson would not have been sure of his grandfather's feelings toward Cicero. And yet Augustus, who allowed Cicero's name to go on the list of people to be killed, also appreciated Cicero's writing and recognized his patriotism.

Love of Rome and a huge literary talent played critical roles in Cicero's life and death, and Augustus was not the only one who was affected by Cicero. Indeed, over the centuries since Cicero's death in 43 BC, many people have come to know of his patriotism, as well as his insecurities, his friendships and loves, and his fears, triumphs, and mistakes. We know more about Cicero than any other Roman of the ancient world, and we know much of it from Cicero himself. Many famous Romans had biographies written about them by others, and we are also lucky enough to have works written by famous Romans themselves, like Julius Caesar's account of his military campaign in Gaul. But with Cicero we have not only the works other historians have written about him, and some of the many speeches he made as a politician and lawyer, but also hundreds of the letters he wrote. Cicero wrote to famous people of the time such as Marcus Brutus, Julius Caesar, and Pompey, but he also wrote to close friends and family. It is in these letters that we learn the most about him and the life of a Roman politician.

A NOTE ON ROMAN NAMES AND DATES

Roman names can be confusing. For example, this book is about Marcus Tullius Cicero, son of Marcus Tullius Cicero, and grandson of Marcus Tullius Cicero. I have therefore called him "Cicero" throughout the book, and his brother is referred to as "Quintus."

Furthermore, throughout the book, in translating dates from original sources, I have always used the modern and commonly accepted BC and AD dates rather than the Roman dates used in the original. It is taken for granted that the reader understands that an ancient Roman writing before the birth of Christ would not have written dates in terms of BC and AD.

ARPINUM

Marcus Tullius Cicero was born around 106 BC, but he was not born in Rome. He was born on his grandfather's farm a few miles from the hill town of Arpinum. Arpinum was seventy miles from Rome, or two to three days' travel away.

CITIZENSHIP

The people of Arpinum were Roman citizens and had been for a long time, so they were more privileged than many of the people living in Italy at the time. Full Roman citizenship was considered very valuable. You had the right to a trial if someone accused you of a crime. You were allowed to vote in the elections that were held every year in Rome. You may have also felt that you were a part, however small, of

The ruins of the Forum in Rome, Italy. During the time of Cicero, the Forum was Rome's major political and commercial center.

the great Roman Empire. Of course it wasn't that simple. No woman could be a Roman citizen and vote, nor could a slave. Even a freed slave was not allowed all the rights of a Roman citizen. And voting in elections was all very well if you had the time and money to make the journey to Rome every year. Theoretically, as a citizen, you could vote to decide who was elected to all the posts of government, even that of the chief priest of the Roman religion. You could vote to decide whether or not a proposal became a law. But Rome was not a democracy because all votes were not equal. You voted with many other people in groups, and the voting power of these groups did not all carry the same weight. Some groups had more people in them than other groups, and some were only for rich people. For example, imagine that the election for the top job, the consulship, is being held, and you join your voting group, which is called a century. You are very rich and so is everyone else in your century. The century next to you is composed of many more people, who are not as rich. Each person in that century will find it much more difficult to make his opinion count.

The people in some places in Italy, such as Arpinum, were given full Roman citizenship as a reward for being helpful to Rome as she had expanded to take over Italy and the rest of the Mediterranean. People of other towns and regions were only given a sort of second-class citizenship, called "Latin status," and much of Italy was even lowlier than that, with the grade "Italian status." These types of citizenship were less worthwhile than full Roman citizenship because they granted fewer rights and opportunities.

It is easy to see why many people who were born and lived in Rome thought of themselves as being superior to anyone who lived outside Rome. It took a long time for urban Romans to realize how this formed a barrier between the city and the empire, even between the city of

Rome and the rest of Italy. At the time of Cicero's birth, this difference in treatment was beginning to irritate those who did not enjoy full citizenship. When Cicero was a teenager, a war broke out over this issue. Someone like Cicero from outside Rome could understand and sympathize with the Italians. He always felt himself to be something of an outsider. He once wrote of Arpinum:

> I shall never deny that this is my fatherland, even while the other fatherland is greater and contains this one . . .

By "the other fatherland" Cicero meant Rome. He was talking about a kind of dual citizenship. Even someone like Cicero, who spent so much of his life in Rome and was deeply involved in

A first century AD wall painting of Roman ships in the harbor at either Stabiae or Puteoli. Trade with Rome's Mediterranean provinces was her greatest source of wealth.

17

This wall carving depicts stages in the life of a Roman boy. On the left he is nursed by his mother while his father looks on. Then he is held in his father's arms. Next he rides in a toy chariot pulled by a goat. Finally he is shown in conversation with his tutor.

its politics, felt that there was a gap between Rome and the rest of Italy. Having this dual citizenship was both an advantage and a disadvantage for Cicero later in his life. He could understand what it was like to be one of the many respectable people who lived outside Rome, and the support of such people helped him a great deal in his career. Unfortunately, to the upper classes born and bred in Rome, Cicero was never one of them, and one even called him "a foreigner"!

CICERO'S FRIENDS

Three people were of special importance to Cicero to the end of his life: his younger brother, Quintus; his best friend, Atticus; and a slave called Tiro. As a slave, Tiro would have had none of the rights familiar to us in our own time. Instead, he would have been legally viewed as a piece of property. He would have been just one of the millions of people who, through capture in war or birth to a slave mother, were slaves themselves. There were probably more slaves than free people in Rome at this time, and anyone who could afford it would have owned at least one slave. Slavery was a part of Roman life. But a slave and a free citizen could form real bonds of

affection, as shown in this letter from Cicero to Tiro:

The messenger told me that you were now free from fever and getting better, but because he said that you were not able to write to me, I got worried—and all the more because Hermia, who was supposed to arrive that day, did not. I really am very concerned about your health. Apply your considerable intelligence

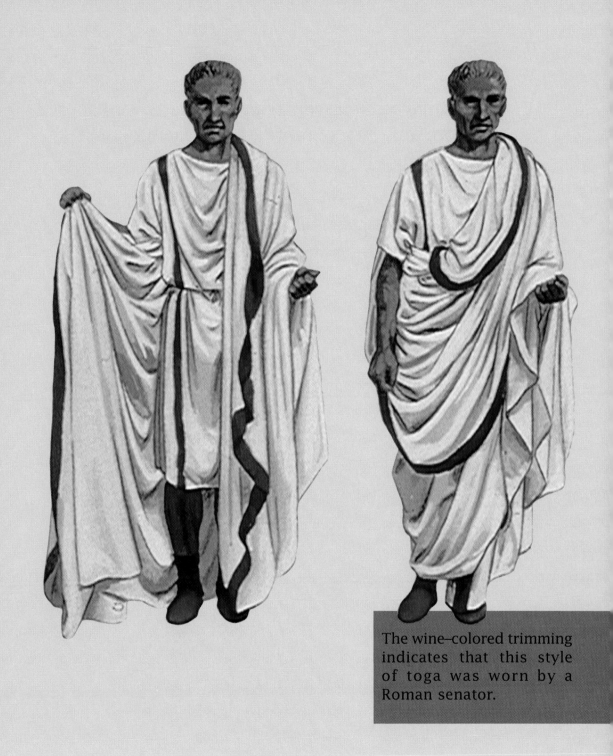

The wine–colored trimming indicates that this style of toga was worn by a Roman senator.

to getting yourself well again for me as well as for yourself. Once more—take the greatest care of yourself.

As you will see, Cicero officially freed Tiro, and he became Marcus Tullius Tiro, Cicero's friend and secretary.

MAKING THE GRADE

Education was taken very seriously in the Roman world, as long as there was money to pay for it. For a family like Cicero's, education was a lengthy business, lasting until the boy was about seventeen and then continuing if he showed that he had talent. Girls might be taught basic skills such as reading and writing, but it was unusual for a girl to receive any formal education beyond that. The main roles for women in the ancient world were the production of a male heir for her husband and the smooth management of the household.

THE BASICS

A young Roman boy from an established, wealthy family would be sent to a school or have his own tutor at home. He would be

This stone carving from the second or third century AD shows a teacher and students in a Roman classroom.

taught to read and write Latin and then Greek so that he could appreciate the great literature of the world. The Romans had conquered Greece in the second century BC and had grown to appreciate the culture and arts of that land so much that the poet Horace later said, "Greece captured her captor."

Greek works of art were very popular in Roman houses, and Greek literature was considered part of the basic curriculum for young Romans. So Cicero and his brother, Quintus, would have learned, by heart, large portions of the works of the poet Homer, the man who composed the *Iliad* and the *Odyssey*, long epic poems telling of the Trojan War and the adventures of the Greek hero Odysseus on his way home from that war. Cicero was inspired by Homer's tales of heroes who placed honor before everything else, and he later wrote to Quintus—using the words of Achilles, the great hero of the *Iliad*, who died rather than face a life without glory—of "that determination, which I have clung to since I was boy, to be the best by far, to outreach the rest."

Cicero and his brother studied the great playwrights, historians, and philosophers of Greece, and Cicero became very interested in philosophy. He would write many philosophical works himself later in his life. "Philosophy" comes from a Greek word meaning "love of wisdom." Ancient philosophers tried to work out answers to some crucial questions, such as "What is goodness?" or "What is the best way to rule a country?" Cicero was a very good student, according to the biographer Plutarch. Here is a story Plutarch relates from Cicero's school days:

> When he was old enough to go to school, he gained quite a reputation with the other boys, to the point where their fathers began coming to the school because they wanted to see for themselves this Cicero and his renowned grasp of his lessons. . . .

THE ART OF PERSUASION

Plutarch also tells us that Cicero became especially good at two things: poetry and oratory. Cicero's poetry has not been preserved apart from one or two lines, but it is no surprise to find that he was good at oratory from an early stage. Oratory is the art of making speeches, and Cicero was considered one of the very best orators Rome ever had. This becomes even more significant when you realize how highly the Romans thought of good speeches.

Nowadays, television and newspaper reporters prefer a politician to be able to make their statements short and punchy, and are concerned that we, their audience, may get bored quickly. Romans viewed things very differently. The ability to make long and intricate speeches was vital to anyone who wanted to make a success of himself in public life. When a politician wanted to

A wall painting of a young Roman reading a scroll, from the city of Herculaneum in the first century AD

get into office, he needed to persuade people to vote for him. If he made good speeches in public places where many people could hear him, his name would become known to a wide audience.

Another way of making a name for oneself before going into politics was to have a career as a lawyer. Any Roman citizen could initiate a prosecution. Indeed, many Romans thought it was their duty to take someone who was breaking the law to court. There was no police force or public prosecutor, and so it was left to individuals to conduct the cases for both the prosecution and defense. Lawyers were also supposed to do this for no other reward than the pleasure of having played their part in upholding the law. In Roman trials, as in modern ones, lawyers for the prosecution and defense had to cross-examine witnesses and make speeches to persuade the jury. Trials were always held in public, so many Romans would attend out of interest, and a lawyer who made entertaining speeches would be noticed by everybody.

Schoolboys were taught how to make speeches and how to phrase their speeches in such a way as to persuade people to do what the orator wanted. This skill is called rhetoric, and it is still important today.

What apart from poetry and rhetoric was taught to a Roman child? Very little in the way of mathematics, geography, or science, but when a boy was about fifteen he would often receive advanced lessons in philosophy and rhetoric, as well as some practical experience as an apprentice to someone already at the height of his career. Cicero probably received most of his

education in Rome, and we do know that he, his father, and his brother, Quintus, moved to a house in Rome to ensure that the boys could benefit from being in

the big city. Cicero was introduced to an experienced lawyer so that he could learn from watching and listening to him. This lawyer was called
Scaevola. He was very old and died during
Cicero's time in Rome. His cousin, also called
Scaevola, then took on Cicero. Being in a circle
of such great men and their friends meant that
Cicero would have met other lawyers, writers,
and politicians.

It was probably at this time that Cicero met
the person who would become his best and life-
long friend, and the person to whom he
addressed most of his letters, Titus Pomponius
Atticus. Links between the Pomponius and Tullius
Cicero families were to be strengthened even further when Quintus, Cicero's brother, married
Atticus's sister Pomponia.

Another possible path for a young man on the
rise was that of military service. Though it was not
compulsory in times of peace, many families considered a year or so in the army to be very useful
for a young man. This did not mean that a wealthy
young man joined the ranks of the ordinary soldiers. He would instead be attached to the staff of
an experienced general and would learn about
commanding men and about the practicalities of
controlling Rome's empire.

In the Roman army, even the ordinary soldiers were well-paid volunteers and Roman citizens, which meant that no one was forced to join up and that every soldier had an interest in keeping the Roman Empire safe and secure. The army was divided into legions of about 5,000 men each. They could be posted anywhere in the empire, to help the governors put down rebellions in their provinces or to carry out attacks on hostile states on the empire's borders.

THE RISE OF SULLA

In the times during which Cicero lived, there were such frequent wars, both abroad and in Italy, that a man had to be very lucky to avoid getting involved in conflict. In 91 BC, while Cicero was still very young, a war broke out between Rome and her Italian allies, who wanted greater recognition from Rome. From 89 to 88 BC, Cicero served on the staff of two generals, Pompeius Strabo and Sulla. This experience, while it does not appear to have brought out any enthusiasm for being a soldier, may have been useful in introducing Cicero to a wider circle of people. Pompeius Strabo had a son the same age as Cicero, and it is quite possible that the two met

An artist's reconstruction of the Theater of Pompey, built in 55 BC by the Roman general Gnaeus Pompeius Magnus

during this time. That son was later to be called Magnus, "the Great One," and we know him as Pompey the Great. Also on Strabo's staff was a young noble called Lucius Sergius Catiline, who was to become one of Cicero's greatest enemies.

Rome's war with her allies lasted until 87 BC, but once the Italian allies were subdued, two great generals, Marius and Sulla, started quarreling with each other. While Sulla went to the eastern end of the Mediterranean Sea to fight King Mithridates, Marius came to power in Rome and managed to get rid of some of his personal enemies before dying of natural causes. For three years, Rome had a very uneasy peace, knowing that when Sulla came back from dealing with Mithridates, it was un- likely that he would be willing to forgive and forget his dispute with Marius. During this time, Cicero was in Rome, carrying on his studies under the famous Greek teachers Philon and Diodotus, and he was sure to have picked up on all the political undercurrents and learned of his elders' concerns about the situation. No one of influence or power could count themselves safe. Cicero wisely kept out of the limelight, preferring to carry on his studies rather than try to make a dramatic entrance into public life. That would come later.

When Sulla did come back in 83 BC, things were as bad as people had feared. Sulla was ruthless in his pursuit of power, and he was backed up by a large and dedicated army. He had himself declared dictator. This gave him authority over everyone else in Rome. For the first time in his life, Cicero saw what could happen when a ruthless individual used the threat of an army to take power. His own teacher, Scaevola, and his cousin, Gratidianus, were killed in the unrest that accompanied Sulla's regime.

CLIMBING THE LADDER

Sulla's return to Rome was marked by violence, but the dictator had a clear purpose in mind. He had a plan to reform Roman politics. He wanted to strengthen the Senate, the body of highborn and wealthy men who discussed matters of state and suggested ideas for new laws. Sulla thought that if the Senate was more powerful, things would get done more quickly and efficiently. He also wanted to change the way the legal system worked by setting up some permanent courts for certain types of crimes.

Unfortunately, Sulla's ruthlessness led to some very dark times in Rome. He had a particularly feared way of getting rid of people whom he thought stood in his way—proscription. Sulla would write out a list of those he wanted to get rid of, and the list would be posted at the Forum in the heart of Rome. As

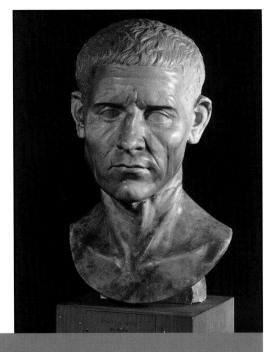

A bust of the dictator Sulla, whose government reforms came at a very high price for Romans

this was the place where the law courts, markets, temples, and Senate House were all clustered together, many people in Rome would pass through it each day. Crowds would gather to read the notices to find out whose name was on the dreaded list. High rank and noble birth were of little help if your name was proscribed. A

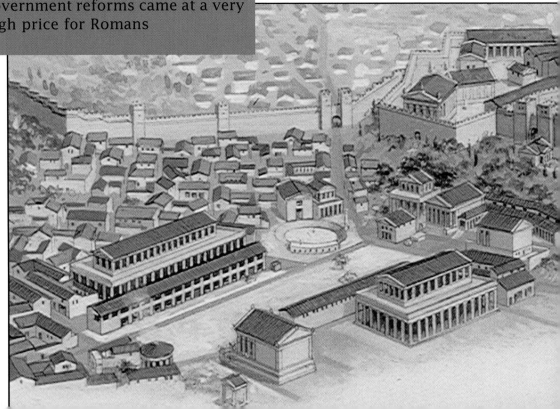

reward was offered to those who carried out the execution of the proscribed person. It gave some people a chance to earn a gruesome living, and others the chance to indulge in personal revenge. Quintus Cicero vividly describes the murder of his cousin Marcus Marius Gratidianus by proscription:

> . . . while Marius was still alive and standing, [his killer] used his right hand to cut off the head with a sword, while his left hand held onto the head. He carried the head in his hand, while between his fingers flowed streams of blood.

The Forum Romanum, the political and commercial center of ancient Rome, as it would have looked around 100 BC

Ruthless people used these terrifying times to their own advantage. In 80 BC, a young man called Roscius was accused of killing his own father, a terrible crime called parricide by the Romans. If found guilty, Roscius could have lost all his inheritance and faced possible execution. Cicero decided that the time had come for a dramatic entry into the world of the Roman law courts and so he defended Roscius. He caused a sensation. Not only did he successfully argue that his client's father had been murdered on the orders of two unscrupulous cousins, he also implicated an ex-slave, a Greek called Chrysogonus. The sensational thing was that Chrysogonus had once belonged to Sulla himself and was still a great friend of the dictator. Cicero had risked offending the most powerful man in Rome in his first important lawsuit! The prosecution had relied on the young and inexperienced Cicero to be so scared of Sulla that he could not defend his client properly.

Cicero, however, was very careful to absolve Sulla of any involvement in the case, while attacking Chrysogonus fiercely. This was a clever tactic because it allowed the jurors to find Roscius not guilty and show their disapproval of the ex-slave without offending his former master. Later in life, Cicero said that he received a lot of praise for this

defense speech and many requests for more speeches:

> And so I gave many more speeches, on which I toiled carefully and perhaps a bit too obviously!

Cicero was being modest, for although his early speeches, like the Roscius speech, were a little florid, they were still very good speeches. The Roscius case was also important for Cicero in that it showed him what he still needed by way of training to become a successful speaker. He traveled to Greece to find the teaching and advice he needed, and it was probably also a good idea for him to take

A photograph of the Curia Julia, the Roman Senate House, which still stands

a break from Rome to let things settle down after his dramatic early success. He was also approaching the age when a young man would be thinking of running for election to the Senate, and he needed to be in top form for that.

BEGINNING A CAREER

To get into the Senate, a man had to be elected by the people of Rome to the lowest office of what was called the *cursus honorum*, the series of jobs that led you higher and higher in Roman politics. If you wanted to become consul, the highest post in the government, you had to have held both the quaestorship and the praetorship first. The aedileship was useful but not necessary. Another job held by many senators was that of *tribunus plebis*, "tribune of the people." Ten tribunes were elected every year, and their task was to keep an eye on the interests of the people of Rome. To do this, they had gained some very strong powers. A tribune was able to propose a law and get a vote held on that law without having to consult the Senate first. He could also stop the Senate from discussing anything if he so wished. This was called the power of the veto. It placed the tribunes in a strange position. They were members of the Senate, and

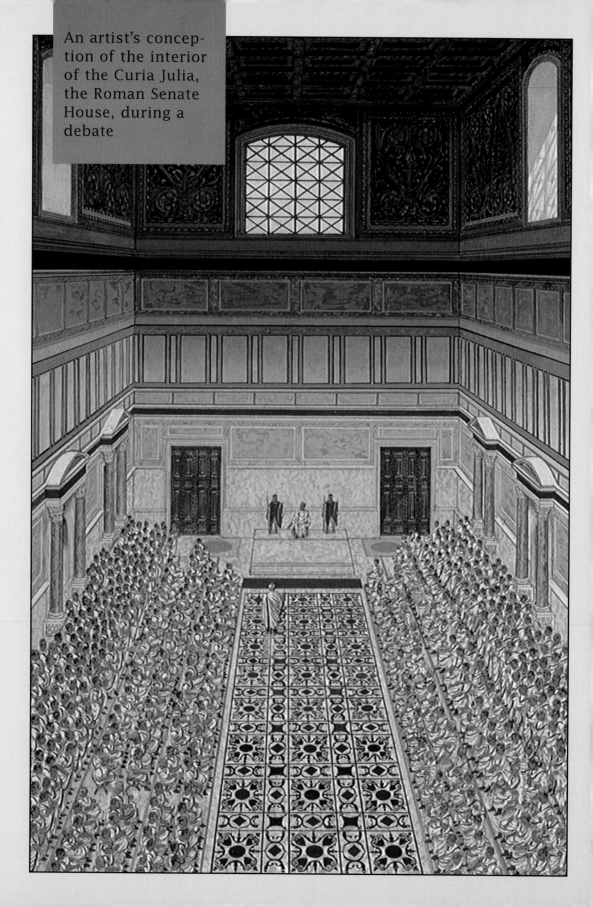

An artist's conception of the interior of the Curia Julia, the Roman Senate House, during a debate

THE *CURSUS HONORUM*

Quaestor

MINIMUM AGE	30
NUMBER	20
WHAT DID THEY DO?	Assisted senior officials in a province or in a treasury

Aedile

MINIMUM AGE	37
NUMBER	4
WHAT DID THEY DO?	Supervised public services like sewers and roads; organized public entertainment

Praetor

MINIMUM AGE	40
NUMBER	8
WHAT DID THEY DO?	Supervised one of the permanent law courts; after a year of office governed a small province

Consul

MINIMUM AGE	43
NUMBER	2
WHAT DID THEY DO?	Supervised Senate meetings, elections, and foreign affairs, and were responsible for Rome's security; after a year of office governed a large province

yet they frequently clashed with the Senate in performing their jobs.

Elections were held in the summer before the job had to be taken up, and voting took place on the Campus Martius (the Field of Mars), an area outside the old walls of Rome, where once the men of Rome had done their military training. In the summer of 76 BC, Cicero went to the Campus Martius and got elected as one of the quaestors for the next year. This was his official entry into the Senate of Rome, and he would be a member of the Senate for the rest of his life.

SICILY AND VERRES

As a very junior member of the government, Cicero's job was to help the governor of Sicily. He went off to Sicily to a town called Lilybaeum (now called Marsala) and seems to have both enjoyed himself and worked hard. Here is his brief description of what he did there:

> I had acquired a large amount of grain at a time when it was very dear, I had been pleasant to the business community, fair to the merchants, generous to the public contractors, unbiased to the allies . . .

The young Cicero was very pleased with himself, but he was disappointed upon his return because few people had heard of him or his work:

> And so I left the province in the expectation that the people of Rome would hand everything over to me. But as it turned out, when I was in Puteoli on my journey back from the province, it was the season when very many of the wealthiest people are usually there, and you could have knocked me down with a feather when someone asked me when I had left Rome and whether there was any news from the city. When I told him that I was actually on my way back from my province, "Oh yes," he said, "Africa, right?" Pretty annoyed, I said in lofty fashion, "No, Sicily." At which, a real know-it-all said "Don't you know anything? He was quaestor at Syracuse." What can one say? I got off my high horse and melted into the crowd of visitors.

But Sicily did more for Cicero than provide him with a neat story to tell against himself. It led to another successful lawsuit. In 70 BC, Cicero was campaigning to be elected aedile, the next post up in the *cursus honorum*. That same year, the people of Sicily sent representatives to Rome to ask for help from the consul, Pompey the Great. They complained that the man who had been governing Sicily for the last three years had been cruel and greedy and they wanted someone to help them prosecute him. They also asked Cicero for help, remembering what a hardworking and honest quaestor he had been when he had worked in Sicily. Cicero took the case, and the ex-governor, Verres, was charged with extortion.

Cicero was up against some strong vested interests. Verres had some powerful friends in the Senate who started to work on his behalf. Verres's allies tried delaying tactics. Cicero traveled to Sicily and collected witnesses and evidence as fast as he could. He was back in Rome before anyone expected him. The trial took place in the summer of 70 BC, and Cicero began with a blistering speech for the prosecution. Verres sneaked out of Rome that night and ran away to Marseilles in southern France. This was a tremendous success for Cicero and meant that he had started his aedileship in a blaze of glory, as a man who defended right against might.

THE CONSPIRACY OF CATILINE

As aedile, Cicero had the responsibility of supervising the markets of Rome. Plutarch says of his administration:

> When Cicero was aedile, the Sicilians, to show their gratitude, sent him lots of the island's produce. He made no personal profit out of this, but used the favor to lower market prices as much as he could.

He also had to organize public entertainment at festivals, and he also kept up his career as a lawyer. By now, Cicero had married. His wife, Terentia, was wealthy and came from a very respectable upper-class Roman family. Making the right marriage was very important for a politician. His wife had to be from the right sort of family.

This second or third century AD stone carving shows a Roman lady being assisted by her maidservants.

Roman women were expected to bring a dowry—an amount of property or money—to the marriage, and a wife's relatives could be useful allies in political life. When aiming for the top, every opportunity had to be exploited. Terentia had given birth to a daughter, Tullia.

REACHING THE TOP

The praetorship was Cicero's next step, and he achieved it confidently in 66 BC. As he explained:

> Three times, thanks to the elections being postponed, I was elected praetor at the top of the polls by all the voting groups.

As praetor, he was in charge of the law court that tried cases of extortion—the very charge that had been brought against Verres four years earlier.

Cicero also made a very important political decision in 66 BC. He supported a move to give a special mission to Pompey the Great. Pompey was currently engaged in getting rid of the pirates who infested the Mediterranean Sea and who had interfered with Roman trade to the point that the price of goods that were transported by sea increased greatly. It was proposed that Pompey should now be sent to Asia, with

A marble bust of Pompey the Great (106–48 BC). Cicero's support for Pompey in the last days of the republic cost him his life.

the job of finishing a war that Rome had been fighting with King Mithridates for years. Mithridates was king of a region called Pontus, near the Black Sea, and he had overrun the Roman province of Asia in 88 BC, sparking off the war that Sulla had fought before becoming dictator. Twenty years later, Mithridates was still a threat. The senators' feelings were mixed. Mithridates needed to be dealt with, but should such resources and powers be given to a man like Pompey? The Senate was worried that he might start acting like another dictator. Cicero, on the other hand, argued that Pompey was the only man to do the job that had to be done. Pompey did get the special mission, and he defeated Mithridates in three years.

Of course, having Rome's greatest general on his side just before he started his campaign for the consulship, the highest office of state, was very useful to Cicero. Cicero was determined to be consul, despite the fact that he was what was called a *novus homo*, Latin for "new man." This meant that no one from his family had held the consulship or even been in the Senate before him. It was very rare for a new man to earn the consulship. How was Cicero going to achieve his aim? To begin with, he checked out his fellow candidates. In a letter to Atticus written in 65 BC, a year before Cicero planned to stand as a candidate himself, he had the following to say:

> The ones I am sure of are Galba, Antonius, and Cornificius. I imagine you are either laughing or groaning at him! And you'll have to pinch yourself when you hear that there are some who think that Caesonius will run! For I do not think Aquillius will run, because he has actually denied it, and he has put in a plea of illness, and his reign over the law courts is in the way. Catiline will certainly be in the running, as long as his trial decides that there is no light at mid-day. I don't suppose you are holding your breath for me to write about Aufidius and Palicanus.

Of the men mentioned in this extract, only two proved to be serious contenders, Antonius

and Catiline. Cicero actually considered defending Catiline in the trial he mentions, but for some reason changed his mind.

Not long after this letter was written, Cicero's son Marcus was born. It must have seemed to Cicero that everything was going very well. He now had a son and heir, which probably did him no harm with the electorate. To the Romans, sons were important, as they would carry on the family name and keep the family's property together.

The next thing a candidate had to do was to get down to some good, hard canvassing for votes. A little handbook of election campaigning, supposedly written by Quintus to his brother, has survived from that time. It is full of tips on how to get votes. Some tips sound as though they might be useful in a modern political campaign:

> The word "friend" is used more widely in an election campaign than in any other aspect of life. Anyone who shows you any goodwill, anyone who seeks you out, anyone who calls at your house, is to be called a friend.

> People from the market towns and country-side think they are our friends if we just know their names.

> You have to use flattery, which even though it is considered a failing and distasteful in other aspects of life, is still necessary in an election campaign.

> Men don't just want promises; they want grand and flattering promises.

> Make sure that gossip gets around, suited to each of your competitors' characters, regarding their misdeeds, scandals, and bribery.

Cicero certainly knew how to blacken the characters of his opponents, going as far as to accuse Catiline of trying to overthrow the state! Romans were allowed to speak much more freely against their opponents without fear of libel lawsuits. The art of invective—insulting someone—was much admired.

His hard work paid off, and in the summer of 64 BC Cicero was elected consul. He took up office on January 1, 63 BC. His fellow consul was Antonius. Cicero seems to have made a deal with Antonius. In return for keeping out of Cicero's way during the year, Antonius got the job of governing an important province the year after. As it turned out, this was a good deal, for Antonius kept his side of the bargain throughout a very eventful year.

A CRISIS FOR THE CONSUL

Cicero ran a very effective spy service as consul and used his spies to keep a close eye on Catiline, the man who had hoped to be one of the consuls. It seemed that he was not taking his defeat in a graceful way, and Cicero soon suspected that Catiline was going to try to take over Rome in a rebellion. Cicero set about trying to gather proof, but it was not easy. He watched the men who were Catiline's friends and recruited an "insider," the girlfriend of one of these men, as an informer. She was called Fulvia, and she would ask her boyfriend, Curius, what was going on and then secretly report back to Cicero. She could not, however, give testimony in a trial. She was a woman, for one thing, and it is unlikely that many Roman senators would have taken her seriously.

Cicero kept watch on Catiline and listened for news outside Rome. As he had feared, there were soon rumors of armed men gathering in the north, in the part of Italy called Etruria. In November, he moved against Catiline, accusing him in a meeting of the Senate of being the mastermind of a fiendish plot against Rome. Catiline denied it hotly, but that night he left Rome and went straight to a place north of Rome called Faesulae, where he joined up with a man called Manlius, who had been in charge of gathering the armed men. The timid Senate at last moved. They declared Catiline a public enemy, and one army was sent to deal with him and Manlius in the north, while another army went south to make sure that no sympathetic southern Italians decided to join in the rebellion. Cicero now turned his attention back to Rome.

Several of Catiline's supporters had been left in Rome, but Cicero did not have any proof of who they were until they played into his hands. He was told about some Gauls from a tribe called the Allobroges who happened to be in Rome on business. They had been secretly approached by men claiming to be Catiline's lieutenants and had been asked to persuade their tribe to join in the rebellion. Cicero asked the Allobroges to play along and persuade the conspirators to give them letters to take back to their tribe. This they did, and the conspirators fell for it. One of them, a man called Volturcius, decided to go with the Allobroges as far as Catiline's camp, where he would deliver a letter to Catiline. On the morning of December 3, 63 BC, the Gauls and Volturcius left Rome, taking the Mulvian Bridge over the Tiber. Cicero takes up the story:

> And so I summoned the praetors Flaccus and Pomptinus, brave men and true patriots. I told them the story and showed them what they must do. But they, feeling all that noble patriots should, without argument and without hesitation took over, and as evening drew near, made their way in secret to the Mulvian Bridge, and there lay in wait in two separate houses nearby, the Tiber and its bridge between them. Without arousing suspicion they had led many brave men there, and I had sent several armed men from the town of Raete, selected young men whom I often use in the defence of the Republic. In the meantime, the third watch of the night was almost over, when the ambassadors of the Allobroges and their party, Volturcius with

them, began to cross the bridge. The ambush fell; swords were drawn by their men and ours. The whole affair was known only to the praetors; everyone else was in the dark. Then Pomptinus and Flaccus intervened, and the fight which had started died down. All the letters found there were handed over to the praetors with the seals still unbroken; the men themselves, under arrest, were brought to me as the day was dawning.

The letters seized that night were damning. Five Romans of high status, including a praetor, Lentulus, found themselves in the Senate on December 4, watching as their letters were opened and read. The Senate praised Cicero, Pomptinus, and Flaccus for their work. There was no doubt of the guilt of the conspirators. The Senate debated the fate of the arrested conspirators for two days and at last recommended in a special decree that they should be executed. Cicero had the five conspirators put to death on the evening of December 5. It is difficult to see what else he could have done, but this would prove to be one of his greatest mistakes.

EXILE

It looked as if Cicero would end his consulship in another blaze of glory, as the man who had saved Rome and had been given the title *pater patriae*, "father of his country," by a grateful Senate. Many people had worked together to defeat the threat posed by Catiline, and Cicero used this to promote the idea of harmony between all the different classes of Rome. He called this idea *concordia ordinum*. But not everyone was pleased.

Cicero himself, as a lawyer, should have been able to foresee the big problem. Under Roman law, every Roman citizen had the right to a trial. The five men executed on December 5, 63 BC, were not given their trial, and objections were raised even before

Cicero left office on December 31. Traditionally, on that date the outgoing consul would make a speech. But Cicero found himself blocked. The new tribunes of the people had come into office on December 10, and one of them refused to allow Cicero to make a speech on the grounds that he had executed Romans citizens without a trial. No one took it any further for the moment, but Cicero knew that this made him vulnerable. This caused him to make another mistake. He was so insecure that he kept reminding

A statue of a Roman magistrate, from the first century BC

everyone that he had saved Rome. His biographer Plutarch says:

> At the time he had the greatest authority in the city but made himself tiresome to many people, not through any bad deed, but by forever praising and puffing himself up, something which many found distasteful. There wasn't a Senate meeting, an assembly of the people, or a lawsuit without one having to listen to him babbling on about Catiline and Lentulus.

The armies sent out by the Senate caught up with the rebels north of Rome, and in February of 62 BC, Catiline died along with his rebellion on the battlefield. Cicero went on with his legal work and bought a very expensive new house on the Palatine Hill, overlooking the Forum where he had made so many speeches in the Senate House and law courts. Pompey had also finished the war against Mithridates in the East, and everyone was waiting for the Great One to come back to Rome in triumph. And at the end of 62 BC, there arose another scandal, which at first appeared to have nothing to do with Cicero. We first read of it in a casual reference in a letter to Atticus:

I suppose that you have heard that Publius Clodius was caught dressed in women's clothes in the house of Caesar when the sacrifice for the safety of the people was taking place, and that he only got out safe thanks to a slave girl. It's a huge scandal, which I know will upset you.

The sacrifice referred to was the Rite of the Good Goddess, a festival celebrated only by women. It was a sacrilege for a man to witness the rites. When Publius Clodius Pulcher, a notoriously mischievous young aristocrat, was rumored to have been discovered at the festival dressed as a woman, many Romans were horrified. Clodius was brought to trial and only through a massive bribery effort was acquitted. But he was not pleased with the person who challenged his alibi at that trial, Marcus Tullius Cicero, who testified that he had seen Clodius in Rome that day. It made Clodius's defense—that he had been miles away from Rome at the time—look a bit thin. From then on, Clodius did not like Cicero and his family. Plutarch adds a very interesting story to explain why Cicero got involved at all:

It seemed that Cicero gave evidence, not out of desire for the truth, but to defend himself against his wife Terentia. She did not like Clodius because of his sister Clodia, whom she suspected of wanting to marry Cicero . . . Terentia was an awkward woman and had a great deal of influence over Cicero so she provoked him into joining her in the attack and testifying against Clodius.

Roman women did not have many of the rights that we would expect a person to have in a modern democratic society. They could not vote, for example. But Terentia reminds us that women had a great deal of influence over their husbands. If Plutarch is correct, her jealousy had a far-reaching effect.

THE FIRST TRIUMVIRATE

For the moment, though, Cicero had more serious matters to concern him. At the beginning of 59 BC, he and other Romans found themselves in a dilemma. For various reasons, mainly having to do with sheer exasperation with the Senate, Julius Caesar had formed an alliance with Pompey the Great and a man called Crassus in 60 BC. The three of them had wealth, military might, and ambition, and they decided to combine all their resources so that they could ensure that each member of the pact got what he wanted without having to go through the usual slow channels. Caesar was elected consul in 59 BC, and when he was in power the three men used his office to run Rome as they pleased. The Senate, naturally, was outraged, and so was Cicero. He was also very upset that Pompey, a man he admired greatly, was a member of this gang of three.

At first the three men tried to get Cicero on their side, but he refused. When he started speaking out

A bust of Gaius Julius Caesar (100–44 BC), Roman general and statesman

against them, they decided to muzzle him and chose Publius Clodius as their agent. For some time, Clodius had been trying to get the office of tribune of the people. Pompey, Crassus, and Caesar supported Clodius, and their support was enough to get him elected. Cicero began to get worried. Suppose Clodius tried to pass a law against him?

This was of course what Clodius intended to do. He became tribune at the end of 59 BC, and when the new consuls came into power on January 1, 58 BC, Clodius got them on his side by giving them good provinces to govern. They did not interfere for the rest of the year. It was the same trick Cicero had pulled in 63 BC with his fellow consul, Antonius.

Cicero started rallying his supporters, but he was out of favor. Everyone was fed up with hearing him go on about Catiline. He went to see Pompey, but Pompey slipped out of the back door as Cicero came in the front. Cicero was in despair. After consulting with his friends, he left Rome one night, like his old enemies Verres and Catiline, and went to Greece before Clodius could move against him. Clodius had proposed a law that if a person had put Roman citizens to death without a trial, that person should be exiled. Cicero's mistake of 63 BC gave Clodius the perfect opportunity. After Cicero left Rome, Clodius not only had the law officially passed but saw to it that Cicero's house in the middle of Rome, on the Palatine Hill, was destroyed. He built a Temple to Liberty on the site because he believed Cicero had not upheld liberty in 63 BC when he executed the Catiline conspirators.

CHOOSING SIDES

Clodius also destroyed Cicero's country houses at Formiae and Tusculum, attacked Cicero's brother, Quintus, and left him badly injured in the Forum, and passed bills allowing himself to form gangs and hand out free grain to the poor of Rome. While this made him very popular with some Romans, the people in power did not like his behavior at all. Pompey and Crassus found that they could no longer control Clodius, and Julius Caesar had left Rome after his consulship to govern the province of Gaul, which is now France. The decision to recall Cicero was made in 57 BC, but it still took more time than Cicero would have liked. Exile was the low point of his life. Reading his letters, it appears that he was not capable of bearing his troubles without an

A fresco, or wall painting, of an entranceway to a Roman patrician's house

unremitting stream of woe. This passage comes from a letter to Quintus:

> My brother, my brother, my brother, were you really worried that out of anger I had sent my people to you with no letter? Or that I didn't want to see you? Angry with you? Could I be angry with you? Oh yes, of course, it's *you* who have hurt *me*, your enemies and the dislike felt for you which have destroyed me, not I that have pitiably harmed you! That praised consulship of mine has snatched you, my children, my country, my fortunes away from me.

In 57 BC, with Cicero's friend Lentulus Spinther as consul and with Pompey once more Cicero's friend, Clodius could not stop Cicero's return. Along with Lentulus Spinther, three other friends of Cicero's—Sestius, Milo, and Cispius—were tribunes. These four men had worked tirelessly to keep Cicero's case in the public eye and had canvassed on his behalf for nearly fifteen months on end. Sestius had even gone to Gaul to see Julius Caesar and plead for Cicero, and he had been injured along with Quintus in the Forum riot. Cicero was now triumphant, but poor and in debt to a lot of

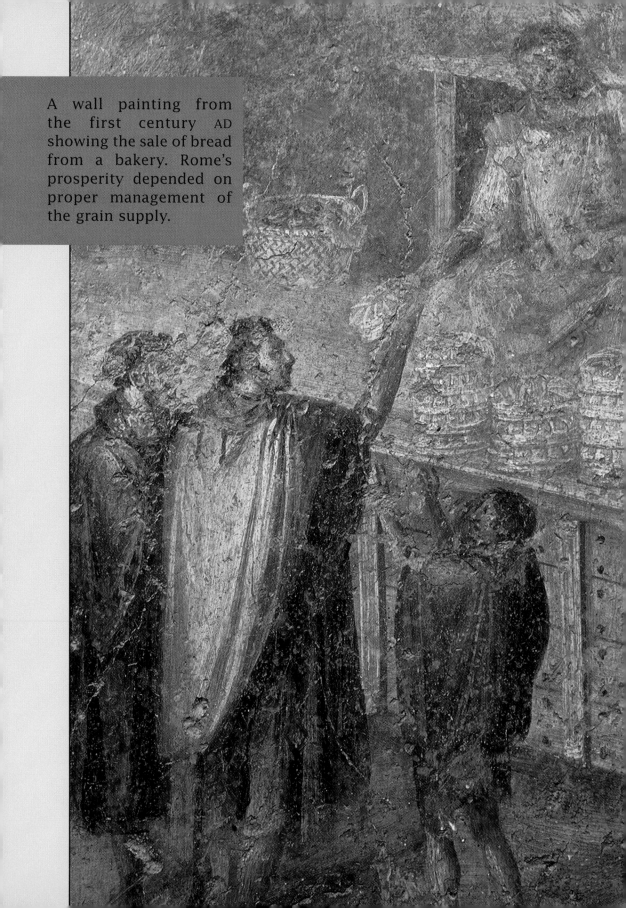

A wall painting from the first century AD showing the sale of bread from a bakery. Rome's prosperity depended on proper management of the grain supply.

people. He began work almost immediately. On September 7, 57 BC, he made a speech in the Senate recommending that the supervision of the corn supply be handed over to Pompey. This was a prestigious and powerful position, made necessary because of Clodius's corn dole, which had practically drained the treasury. Cicero then began the fight to get his house back. The Senate turned over the land to Cicero once more, along with 2 million sesterces to rebuild. This was not nearly enough compensation for a house that in 62 BC had cost him 3.5 million sesterces, but Cicero remained silent about it in public. To Atticus he complained that the senators had been "stingy" when they awarded him 500,000 and 250,000 sesterces for the two country estates destroyed by Clodius's gangs. Cicero was very short of money now, and to make things worse, his relationship with his wife was

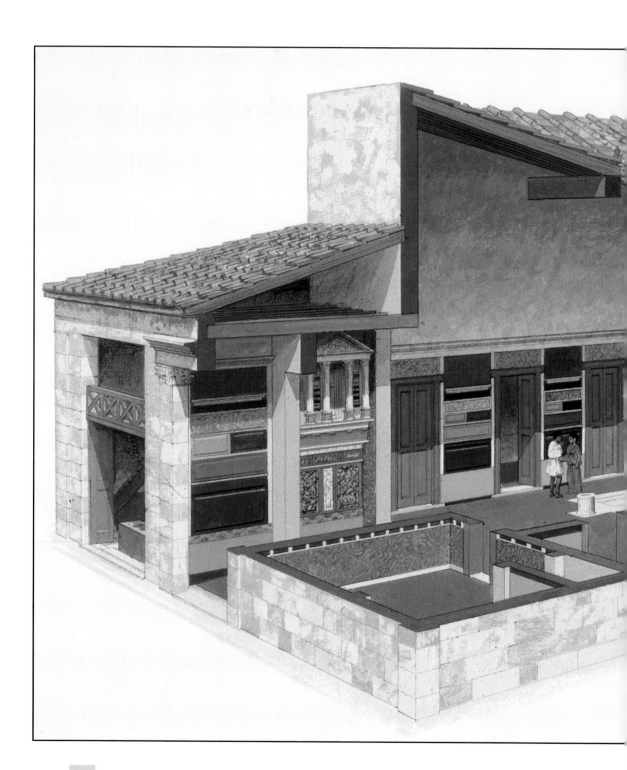

An illustration of the interior of a Roman villa. Usually a series of bedrooms, offices, and dining rooms were grouped around a large hall and atrium entrance corridor.

not going well. At the beginning of October, he wrote to Atticus and hinted as much:

> The other things that bother me are a bit more private. I am loved by my brother and daughter.

Cicero's exclusion of Terentia from this group is quite noticeable!

REVENGE ON CLODIUS

From November 57 BC onward, Cicero got caught up in the running battle between Clodius and the tribune Milo. Milo may have been on Cicero's side, but he behaved similarly to Clodius, forming his own bands of thugs and using just as much violence in retaliation. By this time, Clodius was trying to gain the office of aedile, while Milo was using his gangs to provoke riots in order to delay the elections. It was January 56 BC before the elections were held and Clodius was made aedile. Cicero was kept busy at the start of the year, defending those friends who had fought Clodius when he was in exile. Milo, Sestius, Cispius, and another Cicero supporter, Lucius Bestia, were all charged with one thing or another by cronies of Clodius's during the first three months of 56 BC.

Then, in April 56 BC, Cicero took on an interesting case. A young man who had once been Cicero's student, Marcus Caelius Rufus, was charged with violence, theft, and poisoning. The main witness for the defense was going to be Clodius's own sister, Clodia. Cicero made her the target of an abusive speech. It was a wonderful way of gaining revenge on the whole Clodius family. The charges against Caelius were almost lost in the barrage aimed at Clodia:

> If an unmarried woman opens her home to eager all-comers, and openly lives the life of a prostitute, meeting with men who are complete strangers to her, if this woman does this in the city, in her garden, in the throng at Baiae, if not just the way she walks, but the way she dresses and the company she keeps, not just her come-to-bed eyes, not just her free talk, but also her touch, her kiss, her parties—on the beach, on board her ship, at home . . .

For a Roman woman to be held up to public scrutiny like this was a terrible scandal. Caelius was acquitted.

An illustration of the exterior of a typical Roman country villa. Such houses were at the centers of large estates worked by many slaves.

The Appian Way, the Roman road where Cicero's supporter Milo killed Clodius

CICERO TURNS AROUND

Full of confidence, on April 5, 56 BC, Cicero breezed into the Senate and launched an attack on Caesar's legislation. On the eighth of April, he visited Pompey, who told him that he was off to Sardinia to meet with Cicero's brother, Quintus, about the corn supply. Cicero wrote a cheery letter to Quintus to tell him to watch out for the great man's arrival. On the eleventh of April, Pompey set off, but not for Sardinia. He traveled up the coast to Luca, the southernmost town in Gaul, to meet with Caesar and Crassus. The three men were dissatisfied with the way Roman politics were going and decided they needed to step in once more. Among other things, they decided to silence Cicero. Pompey finally made it to Sardinia, and it was probably there that he told Quintus to convey a message to his older brother that Cicero had to keep quiet. Cicero's brief fight ended. Exile was something he did not dare risk again.

GAUL

Massilia

ETRURIA

ITALIA

Roma

HISPANIA

SARDINIA

SICILIA

AFRICA

Boundaries of the Roman Empire ....

THE ROMAN EMPIRE AT THE TIME OF CICERO

BLACK SEA

PONTUS

PARTHIA

ASIA

CILICIA

SYRIA

ACHAEA

MEDITERRANEAN SEA

Cicero remained out of Roman politics for the next few years. He kept up his legal work and even appeared to defend men recommended by Caesar, Crassus, and Pompey. He was not proud of what he called his "about-turn," but it showed the three men that he was willing to accept their terms. When Milo finally killed Clodius in a clash on the Appian Way outside Rome, Cicero felt obliged to defend him, but he was so cowed that he made a mess of the speech. Milo became one of Cicero's few legal failures.

Sometime around 53 BC, something very important happened in the private life of the Tullius family. Cicero freed his slave-secretary Tiro, and Quintus wrote a letter of congratulations to him. He said:

> I am really pleased, my dear Marcus, about Tiro, that you decided that he was worth more than his status, a friend to us rather than a slave. Believe me I jumped for joy when I read the letters from both of you, and I thank and congratulate you.

Tiro had achieved a new legal status by being freed. There were still some restrictions on him— he could not join the legions of the army, for example—but he was now a Roman citizen.

CIVIL WAR

Legal work and family matters did not mean that Cicero was unaware of the heightening political tension toward the end of the decade. When Crassus was killed while fighting in Asia, there was no longer anyone to keep the ambitions of Caesar and Pompey from clashing. Caesar and Pompey began to move toward a confrontation. At the crucial moment, chance intervened to send Cicero away. A shortage of suitable senior politicians meant that he had to serve a term as governor of the province of Cilicia in Asia. In 51 and 50 BC, while he was away, Cicero used Marcus Caelius Rufus to keep him informed. Caelius sent him very shrewd letters analyzing the situation and discussing the all-important question: If it came to a war between Caesar and Pompey, how did one choose which side to join? Caelius wrote:

> Regarding the crisis of the republic, as I have often written to you before now, I don't see peace lasting another year, and the nearer the clash which must happen, the clearer the danger. This is the sticking point over which the men in power are drawing up their battle lines. Pompey has decided that Caesar

cannot hold the consulship without handing over army and province, while Caesar has decided that it is not possible to leave his army safely; but he offers this condition—that they both hand over their armies. So their friendship and uneasy agreement has come to this—not a secret bickering but full-blown hostilities. And I cannot see what decision I should take—I dare say that this dilemma will be troubling you as well. On the one hand, I have influence and ties of friendship; on the other I hate the men but love the cause.

When a civil war did break out in 49 BC, Caelius chose wisely and went over to Caesar. Cicero found the decision much more difficult because he thought both sides were wrong. He tried very hard to act as a peacemaker between the two men, but neither was interested, and so in the end Cicero went with his heart and followed Pompey to Greece and to a decisive battle at Pharsalus. He must have puzzled Pompey's supporters. He had joined their cause late, found their desire for battle inexplicable, refused to take part in the battle of Pharsalus, and, after the battle, refused to continue fighting. He limped back to Italy as Pompey was fleeing to Egypt. When news came that Pompey had been murdered by the Egyptians as a "present" for Caesar, Cicero fell into despair. One man was now in control of Rome—the sort of rule Cicero had been fighting all his political life, and the complete opposite of his own dream of *concordia ordinum*. He had to wait in Brundisium in southern Italy for Caesar to forgive him for joining the wrong side in the civil war, and it must have been a very anxious wait for him. According to Plutarch, Caesar was generous:

> Caesar when he saw Cicero coming to meet him far ahead of the others, got down and greeted him, and went along the road for some distance talking privately with him. And from then on he treated him with honor and kindness.

Under Caesar, Cicero was allowed to return to Rome, but he felt that once more he had been forced into retirement, unable to fully take part in politics. His Rome did not exist under this dictator. Caesar was away from Rome most of the time but still ran things as he wished. The Senate was kept under control and did what it was told, while Caesar went around the Mediterranean tidying up loose ends and making sure that no pockets of resistance survived.

Last hope

During the years of Caesar's dictatorship, Cicero's personal life was turbulent. After his return to Rome, he and Terentia divorced. They had been married for about thirty years. Plutarch's account makes it clear that people speculated as to why Cicero and Terentia had split up after so long:

He divorced his wife Terentia, after suffering her neglect during the war . . . she emptied Cicero's house of everything and had many large debts besides. These are the most likely reasons given for the divorce, but Terentia denied them, and Cicero himself gave clear corroboration to her by marrying a young girl not long after. According to Terentia he was in love with her youth, but according to what Tiro, Cicero's freedman, wrote, it was because of the opportunity to pay his debts. For the girl was very rich, and Cicero had been made her guardian and trustee of her inheritance. As he owed a lot of money, he was persuaded by friends and family to marry the girl, even at his time of life, and to use her wealth to get rid of his creditors.

It is a familiar story, and Cicero does not come out of it well. The new marriage itself was not destined to last.

Cicero's daughter, Tullia, also had been unhappy in her marriage to a wayward young man called Dolabella, and she divorced her husband at the end of 46 BC. She was pregnant and gave birth in January 45 BC. The birth left her ill, and she died in February. Cicero was heartbroken, as this letter to Atticus shows:

Wanting me to recover from my sorrow is just like you; but you can witness that I am not letting myself down. There is nothing written by anyone on lessening one's sorrow that I did not read while at your place. But my grief defeats all consolation.

Another letter to Atticus reveals how much Cicero missed political life:

This Roman mosaic means *cave canem*, Latin for "beware of the dog."

> What use is a house to me if I can't have the Forum? My life is over, Atticus, and had been over for a long time—it's just that now I admit it, after losing the one thing that kept me holding on.

Without politics, and now without Tullia, life seemed pointless to Cicero. His grief led him to be rather sharp with his second wife, Publilia. According to Plutarch, she did not share Cicero's grief for Tullia. The very young wife could not compete with a stepdaughter who was older than herself and so well-loved. Cicero was not prepared to be understanding, so he divorced Publilia.

Once more his treatment of his wife appears more than a little shabby. One friend who under-stood how Cicero was feeling was Servius

Sulpicius, and he referred to the political situation in his letter of sympathy to Cicero:

> When I received the news about your daughter Tullia's death I was extremely upset, as I ought to be, and I thought it a terrible thing for both of us. If I could have been there with you I would have been where you needed me and I would have told you of my grief in person . . . Nevertheless I decided to write to you a few words, describing what has occurred to me, not because I think these things have escaped you, but because it may be that your perception is not so clear, being blurred with grief . . . Why is it that private sorrow should move you so greatly? Think—how has fortune dealt with us lately? All those things that ought to be as dear to us as children, have been seized from us—country, honor, distinction, every reward of service. What can one more loss add to our pain? Or since we have been hardened by such experiences, shouldn't we have thick skins by now and care less about everything? Or is it for her sake that you grieve? How often must you have thought—as I often have—that, in these times, those who are allowed to exchange life for death have not got the worst of the bargain!

Sulpicius's letter shows us several interesting things about men like Sulpicius and Cicero. They did not feel embarrassed about their feelings and accepted that they should naturally grieve. Their education in Greek philosophy, on the other hand, led them to try to put their own troubles into perspective. The political situation was foremost in their thoughts all the time.

And yet, Caesar's dictatorship cannot be said to have been a complete disaster for Rome. Caesar was an intelligent and resourceful man, and his long years of fighting and command made him used to getting things done efficiently. He carried out many reforms that were of immense benefit to Rome.

Even before Tullia's death, Cicero had embarked on an impressive period of writing. He had composed works on oratory and started a series of translations of Greek works on philosophy. He wanted to form Latin words to express Greek ideas. He went back to writing poetry—up to 500 lines in an evening according to Plutarch—and intended to write a history of Rome.

ANTONY AND OCTAVIAN

When Julius Caesar was assassinated on March 15, 44 BC, Cicero's name was called out by the assassin Marcus Brutus. Cicero answered this call with a return to politics, at the age of sixty-two. The assassins, or liberators as they preferred to be known, had not planned ahead. They had decided to kill Caesar and had thought that things would go back to normal afterward. They had not anticipated the powerful men who came forward to fight over the rule of Rome in Caesar's place—people like Mark Antony, who had been Caesar's right-hand man. There was also Caesar's heir, a nineteen-year-old called Octavian, who turned out to be fiercely ambitious and ruthless.

At first, Cicero watched and waited in some anxiety. He left Rome, intending to visit his son Marcus, who was studying in Greece, but changed his mind. In August 44 BC, he traveled back to Rome and made ready to join in the debate over what should happen. This was to prove his downfall. He began to criticize Mark Antony and to support the young Octavian, who was later known as Augustus. He made a series of speeches that criticized and infuriated Mark Antony, whose vigorous replies ensured that he and Cicero were to become enemies. Octavian, on the other hand, seemed willing to take Cicero's advice and support. He already had the power of being Julius Caesar's heir—many of Caesar's former soldiers, for example, rallied to him—and he now needed support in the Senate. Plutarch says that Octavian went so far as to call Cicero "father"! Cicero thought that he would be able to use the young Octavian against Antony, but others saw the dangers more clearly. Marcus Brutus, one of the men who assassinated Caesar, could not understand why Cicero was so easily taken in by Octavian. Brutus wrote to Atticus:

A Roman coin featuring a portrait of Mark Antony

I know that Cicero has always acted for the best; what could I be more certain of than Cicero's feelings for the country? But in some respects this man, the most careful of all men, has acted in a way which I could call naive or ingratiating . . . I have only one thing to say to you, that Cicero has stirred up rather than calmed the boy's greed and waywardness . . . Let Octavian call Cicero "father" then, let him consult Cicero in every matter, let him praise and thank him—this will become clear, that he does not mean what he says. . .

Brutus, unfortunately, was right. Octavian used Cicero's influence in the Senate to achieve a very high position for one so young. When the Senate decided to act against Mark Antony, Octavian accompanied the two consuls to the battlefield. When the consuls died during the fighting, Octavian was left in command of the army. If anything had been learned by the Senate in the last fifty years, it was that men who command the loyalty of an army are dangerous. On July 27, 43 BC, Cicero wrote a letter to Marcus Brutus, and it is clear that he was beginning to realize what Octavian was like:

> I hope to hold onto him [Octavian] despite the heavy opposition: he seems to be naturally of the right character, but he's at a dangerous age and there are many people ready to lead him astray.

Octavian was not led astray by anyone. He was his own master. He persuaded Cicero and the Senate that he, Octavian, should receive the consulship at the very young age of twenty. Once he had achieved this, he started negotiations with Antony, knowing that Cicero and the Senate were not going to trust him for much longer. Earlier that year, he had heard a rumor that Cicero had described him as "someone to cultivate, elevate, and eliminate."

In November 43 BC, Octavian and Antony decided to join forces with a third man, Lepidus, and form a triumvirate, a rule of three like that of Caesar, Crassus, and Pompey nearly twenty years before. They drew up a list of people who would have to be disposed of, and Cicero's name was right at the top of the list, at Mark Antony's request. Plutarch tells us that Octavian fought to save Cicero for two days but gave way to Antony on the third day.

Cicero and his brother and nephew heard of the threat and decided to flee. They set off for Cicero's house at Astura but decided to split up along the way so that Quintus could go to his house and get some of his things. Quintus and his son were caught and killed. Cicero made it to Astura and started sailing down the coast. He had stopped off at one of his houses at a place called Caieta, and some loyal slaves were trying to hurry him down to the sea in a litter when Antony's men, led by a soldier called Herennius, caught up with him. He told the slaves to stop and waited in the litter. Here is Plutarch's account:

> He put his chin in his left hand, his usual attitude, and looked fixedly at his killers. His hair was a mess and his face was worn with his worries, so most of the people around hid their faces as Herennius was killing him. He stretched his head out from the litter and his throat was cut: he was in his sixty-fourth year. On Antony's orders, his head and hands were cut off, the hands with which he had written the speeches against Antony . . . Antony ordered the head and hands to be placed above the ships' prows on the Rostra, a sight to make the Romans shiver, because they thought they saw not the image of Cicero's face so much as the image of Antony's soul.

EPILOGUE

> Thanks to what I have suffered, I have gained more honor than toil, more glory than trouble, more happiness in the affection of good men than sadness at the joy of wicked men.

So Cicero wrote in one of his philosophical works, *On the Republic*. Whether he still held the same opinion at the end of his life is hard to tell, but the calmness and courage with which he faced death seem to fit in with these thoughts. Because he left behind so many of his thoughts in his writing, we see the flaws in his character very clearly. Cicero is easy to criticize. In modern editions, Cicero's works take up twenty-eight volumes of speeches, letters, and essays. And that perhaps is his greatest contribution to us. He has given us so much information that we can make ordinary criticisms and judgments, such as we make in our encounters with other people every day. Cicero gives us the ability to step just a little closer to the ancient world and see it peopled, not with dry and dusty two-dimensional figures, but with fallible and therefore interesting human beings.

And what of those human beings? What happened next? Octavian and Mark Antony hunted down and killed Caesar's assassins, including Marcus Brutus, at the Battle of Philippi in 42 BC. Antony had one of the most famous love affairs in history, with Cleopatra, queen of Egypt, but the lovers were eventually defeated by Octavian at the Battle of Actium. Antony and Cleopatra committed suicide in Egypt, and the field was left clear for Octavian. He chose Cicero's son, young Marcus, to be his fellow consul in 30 BC, and in that year Mark Antony's statues in Rome were taken down. Perhaps Marcus was gaining a small revenge on his father's enemy.

In 27 BC, Octavian changed his name to Augustus and became Rome's first emperor. He ruled until AD 14. Atticus survived these turbulent times. His daughter married Agrippa, a friend of Octavian, and his granddaughter Vipsania married Tiberius, Octavian's stepson and a future emperor.

Terentia is supposed to have survived to the grand old age of 103, marrying another writer, the historian Sallust.

As for faithful Tiro, he collected and published Cicero's notes and a collection of his jokes, and was possibly the person who edited Cicero's letters. If Tiro was responsible for the letters that survived, he has more than paid back the kindness shown him by the Tullius family, for through the letters they have all gained a kind of immortality.

GLOSSARY

aedile The second step on the *cursus honorum*. It was an expensive job as the person had to pay for entertainment for the whole city out of his own pocket.

century A group of people who all voted together. Centuries were of different sizes, depending on the wealth of the people in each century.

concordia ordinum Cicero's dream of harmony between the classes.

consul The top job in Roman politics. Two consuls held office every year and supervised the day-to-day running of politics in Rome.

cursus honorum A series of jobs that ambitious senators had to hold to get to the highest position possible, the post of consul.

Forum Romanum Usually just called the Forum, this was the heart of Rome. It was a low-lying flat area, where temples, law courts, and the Senate House were all grouped together.

novus homo   A Latin phrase meaning "new man." This term is given to a man whose family has never had anyone in the Senate before.

patrician   A member of a select group of families, which included the oldest and wealthiest in Rome.

plebeian   Anyone who was not a patrician.

praetor   The third office of the *cursus honorum*, usually involving supervision of the law courts.

province   An area of the Roman Empire, ruled on behalf of the Senate and people of Rome by a governor.

quaestor   The lowest step of the *cursus honorum*, usually involving assisting a more senior official.

Senate   The body of men drawn from the upper classes who discussed public business and recommended laws. Technically, the Senate could do no more than advise the people of Rome, but in reality it was extremely powerful.

tribunus plebis   "Tribune of the people." Elected by a special gathering of the plebeians of Rome to look after them. It was a popular office because of its special powers of proposing laws and vetoing Senate business.

veto   A Latin word meaning "I forbid." It was a special power held by a tribune, who could forbid any discussion or transaction of public business.

FOR MORE INFORMATION

ORGANIZATIONS
American Classical League
(National Junior Classical League)
Miami University
Oxford, OH 45056
(513) 529-7741
Web site: http://www.aclclassics.org
e-mail: info@aclclassics.org

American Philological Association
University of Pennsylvania
292 Logan Hall
249 South 36th Street
Philadelphia, PA 19104-6304
(215) 898-4975
Web site: http://www.apaclassics.org
e-mail: apaclassics@sas.upenn.edu

Classical Association of New England
Department of Classical Studies
Wellesley College
106 Central Street
Wellesley, MA 02481
Web site: http://www.wellesley.edu/
  ClassicalStudies/cane
e-mail: Rstarr@wellesley.edu

WEB SITES

Due to the changing nature of Internet links, the Rosen Publishing Group, Inc., has developed an online list of Web sites related to the subject of this book. This site is updated regularly. Please use this link to access the list:

http://www.rosenlinks.com/lar/cice/

For FURTHER READING

Carcopino, Jérôme. *Daily Life in Ancient Rome.* New Haven, CT: Yale University Press, 1992.

Cicero, Marcus Tullius. *Letters to Atticus.* (Loeb Classical Library.) Edited and translated by D. R. Shackleton Bailey. Cambridge, MA: Harvard University Press, 1999.

Cicero, Marcus Tullius. *On Government.* Translated by Michael Grant. New York: Viking, 1994.

Cicero, Marcus Tullius. *Selected Letters.* Translated by D. R. Shackleton Bailey. New York: Viking, 1986.

Cicero, Marcus Tullius. *Selected Political Speeches.* Translated by Michael Grant. New York: Viking, 1997.

Nardo, Don. *The Roman Republic.* San Diego, CA: Lucent, 1994.

Plutarch. *The Fall of the Roman Republic.* Translated by Rex Warner. New York: Viking, 1954.

Plutarch. *Plutarch's Lives.* Translated by John S. White. Cheshire, CT: Biblo & Tannen, 1995.

Shotter, David. *The Fall of the Roman Republic.* New York: Routledge, 1994.

Time-Life Editors. *What Life Was Like When Rome Ruled the World: The Roman Empire 100 BC–AD 200.* New York: Time-Life, 1997.

Wiedemann, Thomas E. J. *Cicero and the End of the Roman Republic.* London: Gerald Duckworth and Company, 1994.

BIBLIOGRAPHY

PRIMARY SOURCES

Cicero, Marcus Tullius. *Brutus.* Oxford, England: Clarendon Press, 1903.

Cicero, Marcus Tullius. *Letters to Atticus.* Cambridge, MA: Harvard University Press, 1999.

Cicero, Marcus Tullius. *Letters to His Brother Quintus.* Cambridge, MA: Harvard University Press, 1989.

Cicero, Marcus Tullius. *Letters to His Friends.* Cambridge, MA: Harvard University Press, 2001.

Cicero, Marcus Tullius. *On the Laws.* Cambridge, MA: Harvard University Press, 1928.

Cicero, Marcus Tullius. *On the Republic.* Cambridge, MA: Harvard University Press, 1928.

Cicero, Marcus Tullius. *Speech in Defence of Caelius.* Oxford, England: Clarendon Press, 1960.

Cicero, Marcus Tullius. *Speech in Defence of Plancius.* Oxford, England: Clarendon Press, 1911.

Cicero, Marcus Tullius. *Speech in Favour of the Manilian Law*. London: Macmillan, 1966.

Cicero, Quintus Tullius. *Handbook on Election Canvassing*. Cambridge, MA: Harvard University Press, 1989.

Plutarch. *Life of Cicero*. London: William Heinemann, 1920.

SECONDARY SOURCES

Bradley, Pamela. *Ancient Rome: Using Evidence*. Victoria, Australia: Edward Arnold (Australia) Pty Ltd., 1990.

Everitt, Anthony. *Cicero: A Turbulent Life*. London: John Murray Ltd., 2001.

Rawson, Elizabeth. *Cicero: A Portrait*. Bristol, England: Bristol Classical Press, 1983.

Shackleton Bailey, D. R. *Cicero*. London: Duckworth, 1971.

Stockton, David. *Cicero: A Political Biography*. Oxford, England: Oxford University Press, 1971.

Syme, Ronald. *The Roman Revolution*. Oxford, England: Oxford University Press, 1960.

Taylor, David. *Cicero and Rome*. London: Macmillan Education Ltd., 1973.

INDEX

ABOUT THE AUTHOR

Fiona Forsyth read classics at Somerville College, Oxford University. She now teaches classics at the Manchester Grammar School, where she has managed to teach Cicero in one guise or another for ten years. She has been accused by her students of being in love with Cicero, but she hotly denies this.

CREDITS

EDITOR

Jake Goldberg

DESIGN AND LAYOUT

Evelyn Horovicz